PIANO · VOCAL · GUITAR

deep BLUES

57 ESSENTIAL BLUES STANDARDS

This publication is not for sale in
the E.C. and/or Australia
or New Zealand.

ISBN 0-7935-6483-2

HAL•LEONARD® CORPORATION

7777 W. BLUEMOUND RD. P.O. BOX 13819 MILWAUKEE, WI 53213

CONTENTS

	Title	Definitive Record Version	Significant Cover Version
88	I'm Your Hoochie Coochie Man	Muddy Waters	Willie Dixon
94	It Hurts Me Too	Tampa Red	Junior Wells
100	Key to the Highway	Big Bill Broonzy	Eric Clapton
105	Killing Floor	Howlin' Wolf	Albert King
108	Little Red Rooster	Howlin' Wolf	Rolling Stones
110	Mean Old Frisco	Arthur Crudup	B.B. King
102	Mean Old World	Big Bill Broonzy	Little Walter
114	Mellow Down Easy	Little Walter	Paul Butterfield
116	Merry Christmas, Baby	Charles Brown	Elvis Presley
118	Milk Cow Blues	Kokomo Arnold	Johnny Shines
128	My Babe	Little Walter	
125	Nobody Knows You When You're Down and Out	Bessie Smith	Eric Clapton
131	On the Road Again	Floyd Jones	Canned Heat
138	Please Send Me Someone to Love	Percy Mayfield	B.B. King
143	Ramblin' on My Mind	Robert Johnson	Eric Clapton
150	Reconsider Baby	Lowell Fulson	Elvis Presley
158	Rollin' and Tumblin'	Hambone Willie Newbern	Muddy Waters
164	Saint James Infirmary	Louis Armstrong	Josh White
153	St. Louis Blues	Bessie Smith	Louis Armstrong
168	See See Rider	Ma Rainey	Snooks Eaglin
174	Sitting on Top of the World	Mississippi Sheiks	
176	The Sky Is Crying	Elmore James	Albert King
171	Smokestack Lightning	Howlin' Wolf	Yardbirds
180	Spoonful	Howlin' Wolf	Cream
182	Sweet Home Chicago	Robert Johnson	Johnny Shines
188	Tain't Nobody's Biz-ness If I Do	Bessie Smith	B.B. King
192	The Thrill Is Gone	B.B. King	Albert Collins
198	Trouble in Mind	Big Walter Horton	Otis Spann
195	Walkin' Blues	Robert Johnson	Paul Butterfield
206	Wang Dang Doodle	Howlin' Wolf	Koko Taylor
202	You Don't Have to Go	Jimmy Reed	Otis Rush

ALL YOUR LOVE
(I MISS LOVING)

Words and Music by
OTIS RUSH

Moderate Blues tempo

All your love I miss lov - ing.___
ba - by,___

All your kiss I miss kiss - ing.___
I have in store for you.___

All your love I miss lov - ing.___
All my love ___ pret - ty ba - by,___

5

6

BABY PLEASE DON'T GO

Words and Music by
JOE WILLIAMS

MCA music publishing

BABY, WHAT YOU WANT ME TO DO

By JIMMY REED

Moderately slow

1 You got me run - nin'   You got me hid - in'   You got me
2   up,   Go - in' down,   Go - in'
3 peep - in'   Got me hid - in'   Got me

run, hide, hide, run,   a - ny way you wan-na, let it roll___
up, down, down, up,   a - ny way you wan-na, let it roll___
peep, hide, hide, peep, a - ny way you wan-na, let it roll___

BACK DOOR MAN

By WILLIE DIXON

BLUES BEFORE SUNRISE

Words and Music by
LEROY CARR

Slow Blues

Blues be-fore sun - rise, _____ tears stand-in' in my eyes. _____
No - bod - y knows _____ what a _____ shape I'm in. _____
Lost ev - 'ry - thing, _____ ev - 'ry-thing I ev - er

owned. _____ I

Blues be-fore sun - rise with tears stand-in' in my eyes. _____
No - bod - y knows _____ what a _____ shape I'm in. _____
lost ev - 'ry - thing, _____ ev - 'ry-thing I ev - er

BLUEBIRD

By JOHN LEE HOOKER

BLUES WITH A FEELING

By WALTER JACOBS

BOOGIE CHILLEN NO. 2

Words and Music by JOHN LEE HOOKER
and BERNARD BESMAN

CHECKIN' UP ON MY BABY

By SONNY BOY WILLIAMSON

CALDONIA
(WHAT MAKES YOUR BIG HEAD SO HARD?)

Words and Music by
FLEECIE MOORE

Medium boogie woogie tempo

don - ia! ___   Cal - don - ia! ___   What Makes Your Big Head So Hard?

CONFESSIN' THE BLUES

Words and Music by JAY McSHANN
and WALTER BROWN

37

GOING DOWN SLOW

By J.B. ODEN

Slow Blues tempo

I've had my ___ fun,   Lord, I can't be ___ low no

more. ___

Ain't got no mon-ey; none of my friends ___ can be

found. ___

Please ___ write my moth-er, Lord, and tell her the shape I'm

in. ___

CROSSROADS
(CROSS ROAD BLUES)

Words and Music by
ROBERT JOHNSON

2. I went down to the crossroad, tried to flag a ride.
Down to the crossroad, tried to flag a ride.
Nobody seemed to know me. Everybody passed me by.

3. When I'm goin' down to Rosedale, take my rider by my side.
Goin' down to Rosedale, take my rider by my side.
We can still barrelhouse, baby, on the riverside.

4. You can run, you can run. Tell my friend, boy, Willie Brown.
Run, you can run. Tell my friend, boy, Willie Brown.
And I'm standin' at the crossroad. Believe I'm sinkin' down.

EVERYDAY
(I HAVE THE BLUES)

By PETER CHATMAN

52

EVIL
(IS GOING ON)

Words and Music by
WILLIE DIXON

FIVE LONG YEARS

Words and Music by
EDDIE BOYD

GOOD MORNING LITTLE SCHOOLGIRL

By SONNY BOY WILLIAMSON

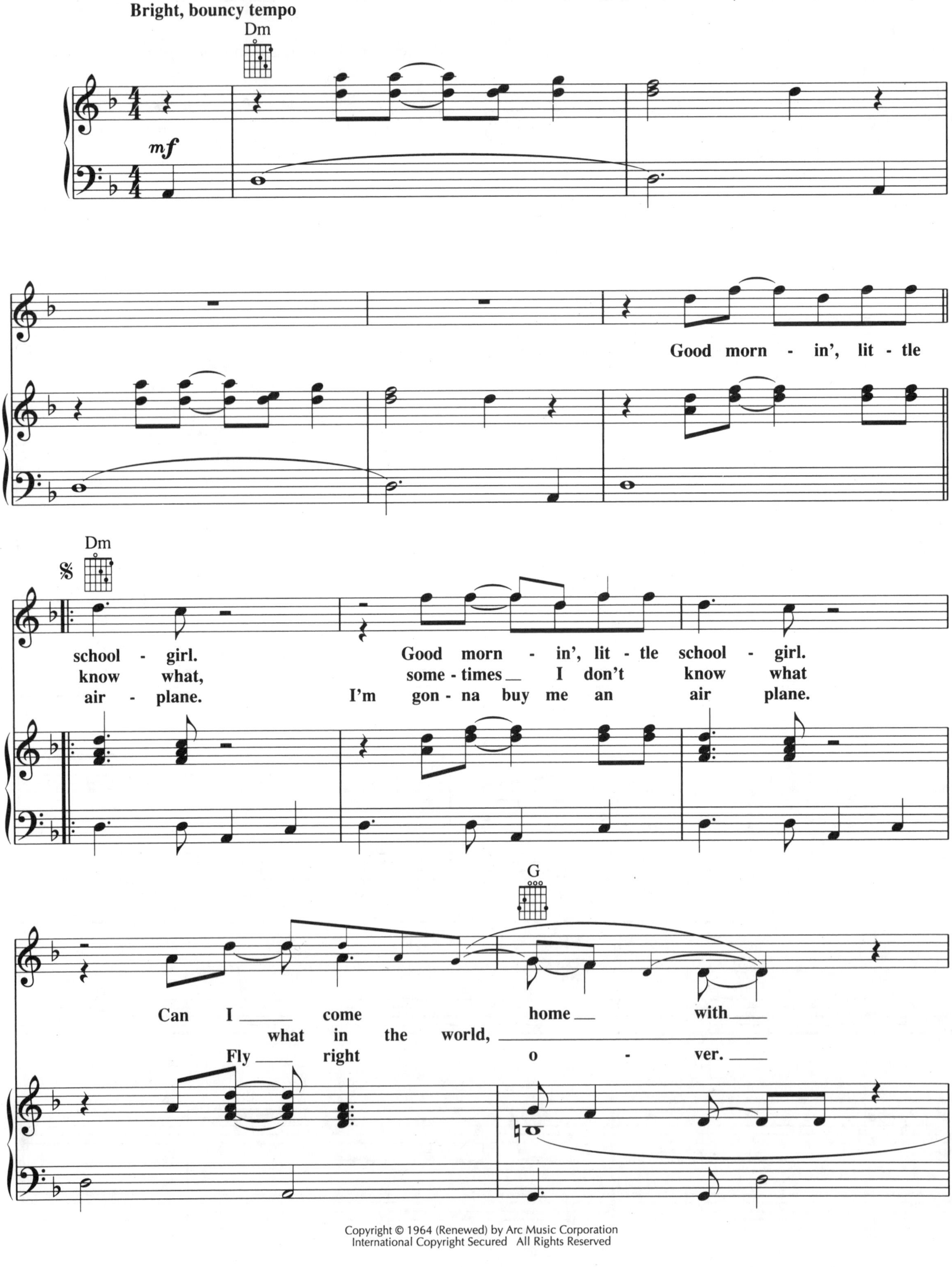
Bright, bouncy tempo
Dm
mf
Good morn - in', lit - tle
Dm
school - girl. Good morn - in', lit - tle school - girl.
know what, some - times I don't know what
air - plane. I'm gon - na buy me an air plane.
G
Can I come home with
what in the world,
Fly right o - ver.

I'm gon- na buy me an

HELP ME

By SONNY BOY WILLIAMSON
and RALPH BASS

HONEST I DO

By JIMMY REED
and EWART G. ABNER, JR.

HOW LONG, HOW LONG BLUES

Words and Music by
LEROY CARR

Additional Choruses (Ad lib.)

If I could holler like a Mountain Jack,
I'd go up on the mountain and call my baby back,
How long, how long, how long.

I went up on the mountain looked as far as I could see,
The { man / woman } had my { woman / man } and the blues had poor me,
How long, how long, how long.

I can see the green grass growing on the hill,
But I ain't seen the green grass on a dollar bill,
For so long, so long, baby so long.

If you don't believe I'm sinkin' see what a hole I'm in,
If you don't believe me baby, look what a fool I've been,
Well, I'm gone how long, baby, how long.

I'm goin ' down to Georgia, been up in Tennessee,
So look me over, Baby, the last you'll see of me,
For so long, so long, baby so long.

The brook runs into the river, the river runs into the sea,
If I don't run into my baby, a train is goin' to run into me,
How long, how long, how long.

I BELIEVE I'LL DUST MY BROOM

Words and Music by
ROBERT JOHNSON

Medium Shuffle tempo

I CAN'T QUIT YOU BABY

Words and Music by
WILLIE DIXON

got-ta put you down _ for a - while. ____

Well, _ I love you ba-by, _ you know you're my on - ly child. ____

Additional Lyrics

2. Well, you know I love you baby-my love for you I can never hide.
   Well, you know I love you baby-my love for you I can never hide.
   Well, I can't quit you baby, my love for you I can never hide.

3. When you hear me moanin' and groanin' baby-you know it hurts me
      deep down inside.
   When you hear me moanin' and groanin' baby-you know it hurts me
      deep down inside.
   When you hear me moanin' baby, you know you're my one desire.

I'M A MAN

Words and Music by
ELLAS McDANIEL

82

I'M A STEADY ROLLIN' MAN
(STEADY ROLLIN' MAN)

Words and Music by
ROBERT JOHNSON

Moderate Rock Blues

I'M YOUR HOOCHIE COOCHIE MAN

Words and Music by
WILLIE DIXON

The gyp-sy wom-an told my moth-er
I got a black cat's bone, _
On the sev-enth hour, _

be-fore I was born, _
I got a mo-jo too, __
and on the sev-enth day, __

you got a boy-child com-ing, he's gon-na be a son-of-a-gun.__
I'm John the Con-quer-or, _____ I'm gon-na mess with you. __
on the sev-enth month, _ the sev-en doc-tors say. __

He's gon - na make   pret - ty wom - en,   he's   gon - na make 'em jump and shout.
I'm gon - na make you pret - ty girls _____   lead   me   by the   hand.
He was born _____ for good luck   and   that   you're   gon - na   see.

Then the world   could   know   what   this was all a - bout. _
Then the world   will   know   I'm the hoo-chie coo-chie man. _   Lord, _ I'm
I've got sev - en hun-dred dol-lars, ba-by, _   don't   you _ mess with me. _

Bb7

here, _   oh   yeah, _   ev - 'ry - bod - y   knows _ I'm

I'M GONNA MOVE ON THE OUTSKIRTS OF TOWN

Words by ANDY RAZAF and WILLIAM WELDON
Music by WILLIAM WELDON

Additional Choruses (Ad lib.)

Chorus 3:
It may sound funny, honey,
As funny as can be,
If we have any children,
I want them all to look like me,
When we move way out on the outskirts of town,
I don't want nobody who's always hangin' 'round.

Chorus 4:
Folks are always callin',
Never seem to let us be,
Makin' new arrangements,
We're not havin' company,
When we move way out on the outskirts of town,
Free from all the people who keep on hangin' 'round.

Chorus 5:
There is no bus or trolley,
And it's too far for a car,
House hasn't got a number there,
They won't know where we are,
When we move way out on the outskirts of town,
Miles from busybodies who keep buzzin' around.

Chorus 6:
So crazy 'bout you honey,
May seem selfish as can be,
Even live in the poorhouse,
If it was just for you and me,
When we move way out on the outskirts of town,
'Way from all your family who keep hangin' 'round.

IT HURTS ME TOO

By MEL LONDON

I'M READY

By WILLIE DIXON

KEY TO THE HIGHWAY

Words and Music by BIG BILL BROONZY
and CHAS. SEGAR

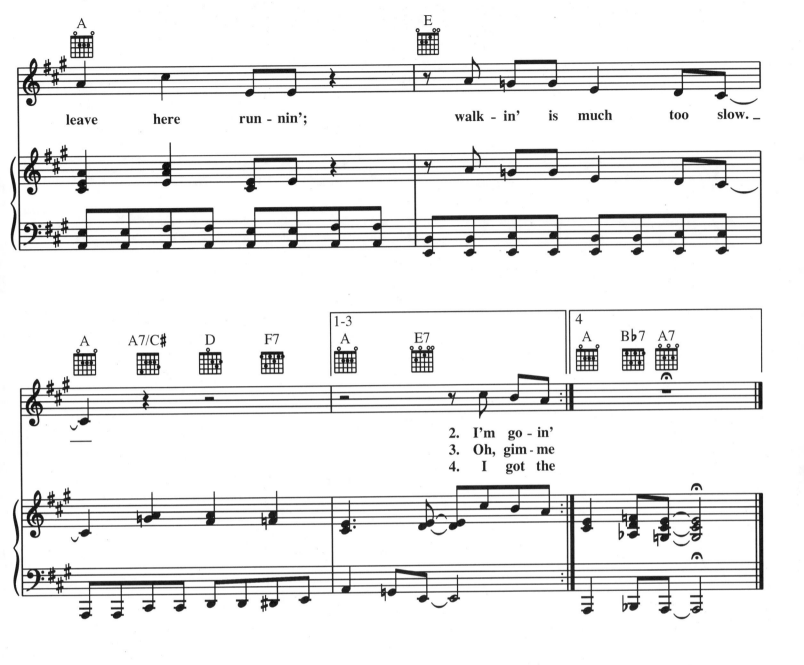

Additional Lyrics

2. I'm goin' back to the border
    Where I'm better known.
    Though you haven't done nothin',
    Drove a good man away from home.

3. Oh, gimme one more kiss, mama,
    Just before I go,
    'Cause when I leave this time,
    I won't be back no more.

4. *Repeat Verse 1*

MEAN OLD WORLD

By WALTER JACOBS

KILLING FLOOR

By CHESTER BURNETT

Moderate Blues tempo

I should-a

LITTLE RED ROOSTER

Written by
WILLIE DIXON

MEAN OLD FRISCO

Words and Music by
ARTHUR CRUDUP

MELLOW DOWN EASY

Words and Music by
WILLIE DIXON

115

MERRY CHRISTMAS, BABY

Words and Music by LOU BAXTER
and JOHNNY MOORE

MILK COW BLUES

Words and Music by
KOKOMO ARNOLD

MCA music publishing

when you won't do right your - self? _____

How can I do right, ba - by,

when you won't do right your - self? _____

If my good gal quits me,

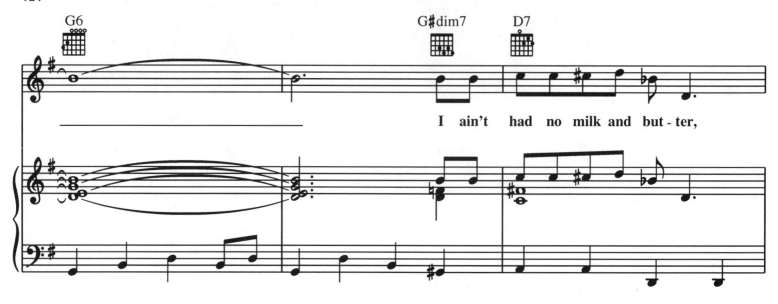

I ain't had no milk and but-ter,

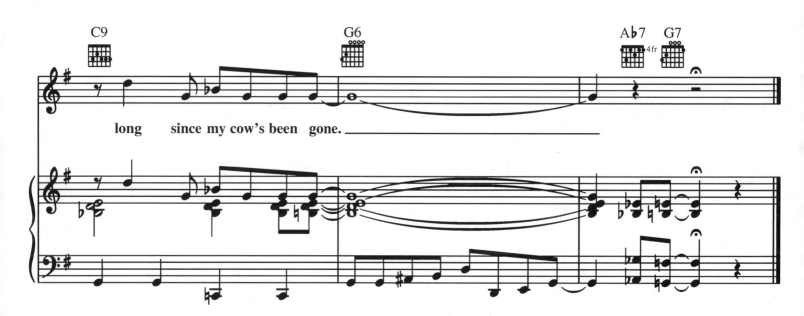

long since my cow's been gone.

Additional Lyrics

My blues fell this mornin' and my love came falling down,
My blues fell this mornin' and my love came falling down,
I may be a low-down dog, mama, but please don't dog me around.

It takes a rockin' chair to rock, a rubber ball to roll,
Takes a long, tall, sweet gal to satisfy my soul,
Lord, I don't feel welcome, no place I go,
'Cause the woman I love done throwed me from her door.

NOBODY KNOWS YOU WHEN YOU'RE DOWN AND OUT

Words and Music by
JIMMIE COX

MCA music publishing

you have-n't an - y. And soon as you get on your feet a - gain, __

ev - 'ry-bod-y is your long lost friend.__ It's might-y strange, with -

out a doubt, __ but no - bod-y wants you __ when you're down and out. __

No - bod - y wants you __ when you're down and out. __ down and out. __

MY BABE

By WILLIE DIXON

ON THE ROAD AGAIN

Words and Music by ALAN WILSON
and FLOYD JONES

Medium Shuffle tempo

Well, I'm so tired of cry - in', but I'm out on the road a - gain, I'm on the road a - gain. Well, I'm so tired of cry - in', but I'm

PLEASE SEND ME SOMEONE TO LOVE

Words and Music by
PERCY MAYFIELD

Hea - ven, ____ please send ____ to all man-

kind, ____ un - der - stand - ing ____ and ____ peace of

mind. ____ But, if it's not ask - ing too much, _

140

RAMBLIN' ON MY MIND

Words and Music by
ROBERT JOHNSON

RECONSIDER BABY

Words and Music by
LOWELL FULSON

ST. LOUIS BLUES

Words and Music by
W.C. HANDY

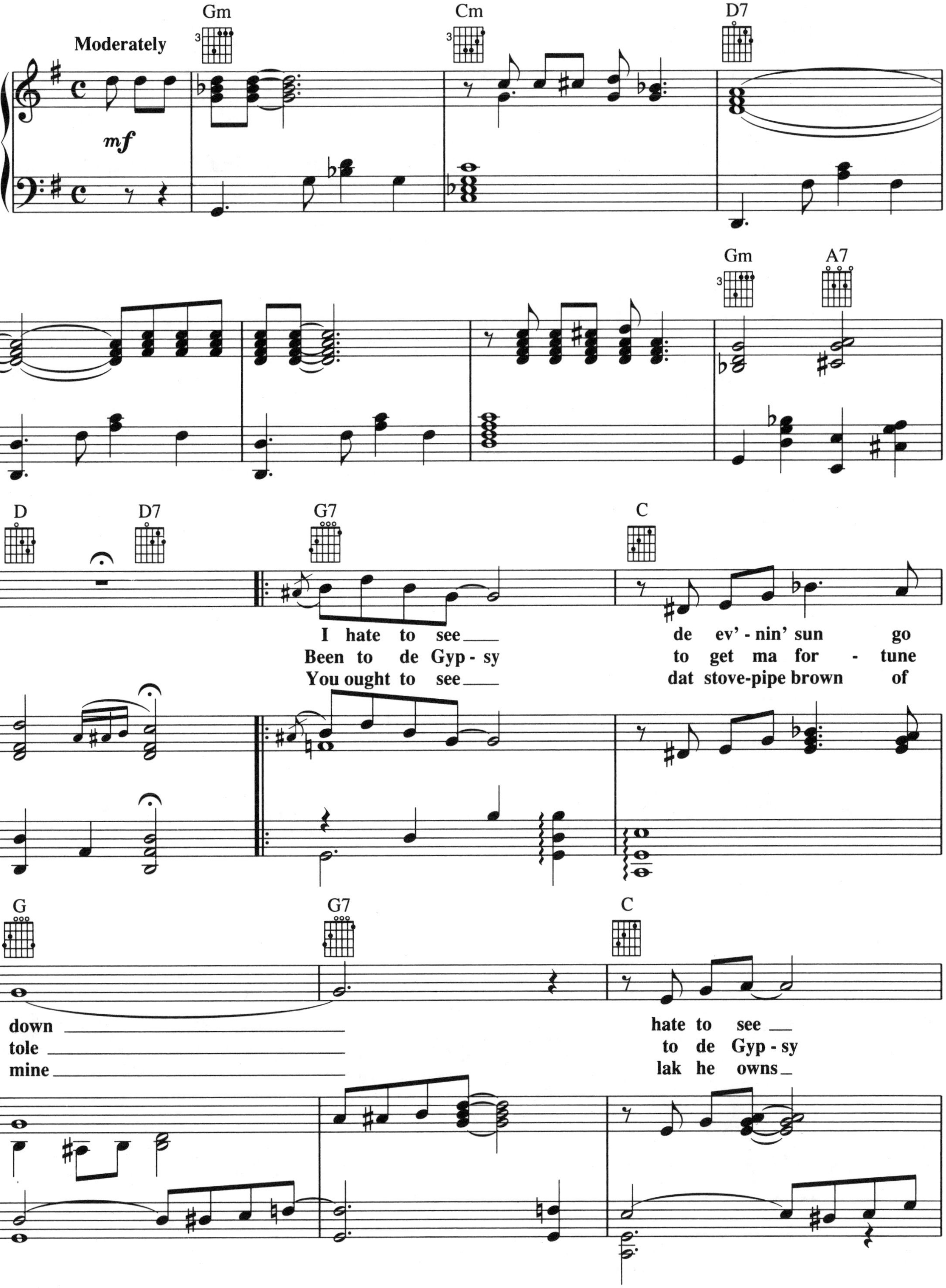
Moderately
mf
Gm
Cm
D7
Gm
A7
D
D7
G7
C
I hate to see de ev' - nin' sun go
Been to de Gyp - sy to get ma for - tune
You ought to see dat stove-pipe brown of
G
G7
C
down hate to see
tole to de Gyp - sy
mine lak he owns

Extra Choruses (optional)

Lawd, a blonde-headed woman makes a good man leave the town,
I said a blonde-headed woman makes a good man leave the town,
But a red-head woman makes a boy slap his papa down.

O ashes to ashes and dust to dust,
I said ashes to ashes and dust to dust,
If my blues don't get you my jazzing must.

ROLLIN' AND TUMBLIN'

Written by
MUDDY WATERS

159

Guitar solo

163

Repeat ad lib.

Solo ends

SAINT JAMES INFIRMARY

Words and Music by
JOE PRIMROSE

SEE SEE RIDER

Words and Music by
MA RAINEY

SMOKESTACK LIGHTNING

By CHESTER BURNETT

Moderately

Smoke, _____ smoke - stack light - ning,
_____ tell me, ba - by,
_____ tell me, ba - by,

shin - ing just like gold? _____ Well,
what's the mat - ter just like here? _____ Well,
where did you stay last night? _____ Well,

don't you hear me cry - ing, boo -
don't you hear me cry - ing, boo -
don't you hear me cry - ing, boo

SITTING ON TOP OF THE WORLD

By CHESTER BURNETT

Slowly

One sum-mer day _____ she went a-way, _____ gone and left me _____ gone to stay, she's gone _____ but I don't wor-ry _____ 'cos I'm

THE SKY IS CRYING

By ELMORE JAMES

SPOONFUL

Words and Music by
WILLIE DIXON

SWEET HOME CHICAGO

Words and Music by
ROBERT JOHNSON

TAIN'T NOBODY'S BIZ-NESS
IF I DO

Words and Music by PORTER GRAINGER
and EVERETT ROBBINS

MCA music publishing

190

THE THRILL IS GONE

Words and Music by ROY HAWKINS
and RICK DARNELL

WALKIN' BLUES

Words and Music by
ROBERT JOHNSON

TROUBLE IN MIND

Words and Music by
RICHARD M. JONES

YOU DON'T HAVE TO GO

By JIMMY REED

204

CHORUS

WANG DANG DOODLE

Written by
WILLIE DIXON

208

Additional Lyrics

3. Tell Fats and Washboard Sam that everybody gon' jam.
Tell Shakin' Boxcar Joe, we got sawdust on the flo'.
Tell Peg and Caroline Din', we gonna have a heck of a time.
And when the fish scent fills the air, there'll be snuff juice everywhere.
To Chorus